The Civil War

by Virginia Slachman

TABLE OF CONTENTS

TEACHER'S GUIDE AND ANSWERS

This book is designed to help students think critically about the Civil War. Themes that run throughout the pages include the differing economies of the North and South, strengths and weaknesses of the North and South, the congressional picture throughout the Civil War, and Lincoln's contributions as a leader and advocate of clemency.

Use these activities to supplement your textbook or to highlight events of the Civil War. Worksheets can be used to stimulate discussion, as in-class work or homework, or as starting points for in-depth study of or research on the Civil War. Class projects might include mock Senate speeches for and against slavery and secession, or speeches written in the spirit of the Emancipation Proclamation or Gettysburg Address to be delivered at a Civil War battle site.

Most pages contain questions that challenge students to think critically about events that occurred during the Civil War. Events are presented chronologically, so activities are most effective if used in order. Page 17 reviews major events covered on previous pages. Page 20 provides students with a comprehensive crossword puzzle on Civil War people, places, and events.

Answers

Page 1

1. Southerners believed their crops and their lifestyles depended upon the existence of slavery.
2. Cotton was very important in the South. Many believed it "ruled" the Southern economy.
3. Because of its large population, the North had many more representatives in the House than the South did. In the Senate, where each state has two representatives, representation was evenly divided. Southern politicians only needed to sway a few Northern senators in order to win a vote.

Page 2

1. *Emancipate* means to free someone or something.
2. According to Tallmadge's proposal, Missouri would essentially be admitted as a free state. With its admittance, there would have been more free states than slave states.
3. An imbalance would favor the opposition and allow them to win legislation.
4. If Missouri were admitted as a slave state as it requested and Maine were admitted as a free state, the balance between slave states and free states would be maintained.

Page 3

1. The Dred Scot decision stated that because slaves were property, they were protected by the Fifth Amendment. Congress, therefore, could not outlaw slavery in any part of the United States.
2. Answers will vary. Students should be able to provide arguments to support their decisions.

Page 4

1. Southerners believed they would have European support because of the European demand for cotton.
2. John Brown's actions stirred up abolitionist sentiment in many Northerners. In many Southerners, it created fear of slave uprisings.
3. Answers will vary. Students should support their opinions.

Page 5

1. Buchanan was weak and had not threatened to force Southern states to remain in the Union. Lincoln, who many viewed as a stronger leader, had not yet taken office.
2. Answers will vary. Students should note that most Southern plantation owners would benefit from secession and the retention of slavery.

Page 6

1. Fort Sumter contained Union troops. The fort was in South Carolina territory which was no longer part of the Union.
2. He did not want the act to appear aggressive or warlike.
3. Answers will vary. Students should support their answers.
4. Answers will vary.

Page 7

Answers will vary.

Answers

Page 8

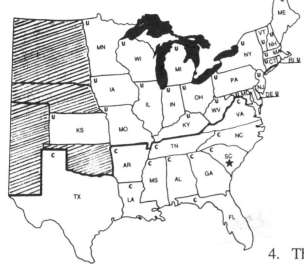

Page 9
1. The *Monitor* was built to stop the *Merrimack*, and it did.
2. Students' articles will vary. Encourage students to answer the questions *who*, *what*, *where*, *when*, and *why* in their articles.

Page 10
1. Many of the Southern slaves who were freed by the proclamation headed north and joined Union troops in the fight against slavery.
2. Students should note that the proclamation caused many plantation owners to lose the slaves who made the plantations productive and profitable.

Page 12
1. November 1863
2. Answers will vary but students should acknowledge that Lincoln was referring to a nation without slavery, and that his hope was to bring the Southern states, free from slavery, back into the Union.
3. He was encouraging the North to continue fighting for the causes that the Union soldiers who were killed at Gettysburg had been fighting for—to abolish slavery and to bring the South back into the Union.

4. The United States Constitution was drawn up by U.S. citizens, approved by U.S. citizens, and created to protect U.S. citizens.
5. a democracy
6. Answers will vary but may include the fact that Lincoln had great regard for the forefathers of the United States who originally conceived of one large nation in which all people are created equal.
7. Answers will vary.

Page 13
Answers will vary. Students should demonstrate an understanding of the fears, courage, and conviction of those who traveled and worked the Underground Railroad.

Page 14
1. Lincoln gave General Grant command of all Union troops which led to the end of the Civil War. Also, Sheridan and Sherman had waged successful campaigns in the South.
2. George McClellan seemed to value peace more than the principle of national unity, and he had not proved to be a decisive military commander. Student opinions will vary.
3. Answers will vary, but students should support their answers.

Answers

Page 15

1. Answer will vary but students should note that the persistence of Grant's attack led to a victory in Richmond and the surrender of General Lee and confederate troops.
2. The defeated Confederate troops would need their horses for farming as they returned to their land and attempted to make their farmland productive once again.
3. Answers will vary, but students should note that the Civil War required men who were once countrymen to fight one another. Some men fought against friends and/or relatives.

Page 16

1. Lincoln's reconstruction plan was charitable and lenient.
2. Answers will vary.

Page 17

1. 5, 6, 4, 1, 3, 7, 2
2. Alabama, Arkansas, Florida, Georgia, Louisiana, Mississippi, North Carolina, Tennessee, Texas, and Virginia
3. Abraham Lincoln delivered the Emancipation Proclamation in 1862. Effective January 1, 1863, it freed the slaves in territories still fighting the Union.
4. Generals Grant and Lee were involved in the surrender at Appomattox Court House.
5. Dred Scott was a Missouri slave who was taken to Illinois and Wisconsin Territory, free areas, and then returned to Missouri. He sued his owners for freedom. The Supreme Court decision denied Scott's freedom and rendered the Missouri Compromise unconstitutional.
6. The Fugitive Slave Law of 1850 stipulated that warrants could be issued for the arrest of runaway slaves in any territory. It also imposed heavy punishment on anyone who aided a runaway slave.
7. Missouri would enter the Union as a slave state, Maine would enter as a free state, and no further slavery would be allowed north of the 36° 30' parallel in the remaining area of the Louisiana Purchase.

Page 19

1. Southerners had to declare their allegiance to the United States.
2. Thaddeus Stevens and Charles Sumner
3. The Radical Republicans were harsh and vindictive toward the South.
4. Congress
5. *Impeachment* is the removal of an official from office.
6. No, he was acquitted shortly before his term as president expired.
7. General Ulysses S. Grant was the next presidential candidate.
8. Lincoln's Emancipation Proclamation only protected people in the South against slavery and this was a temporary wartime policy. Amendment 13 protects all people in the United States.
9. Amendment 15 protects the right to vote.

Page 20

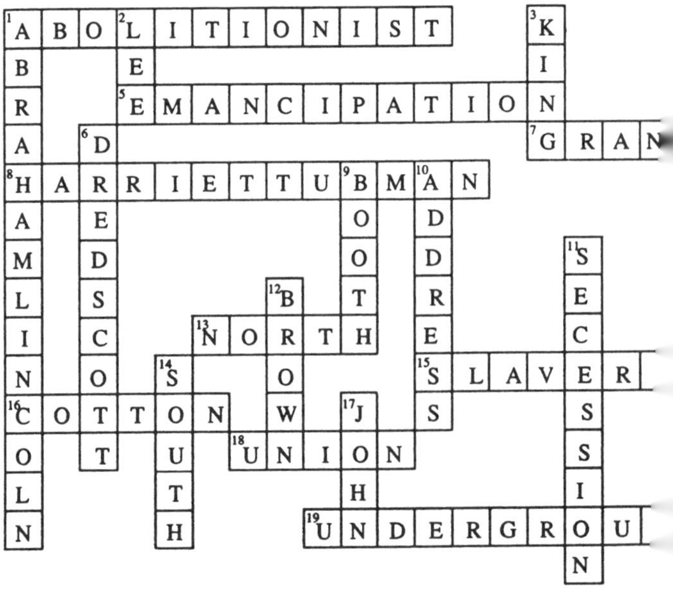

1 ABOLITIONIST
3 K
5 EMANCIPATION
7 GRAN
8 HARRIETTUBMAN
13 NORTH
15 SLAVER
16 COTTON
18 UNION
19 UNDERGROU

The Division

Prior to the Civil War, the North and South were becoming increasingly distinct parts of the United States. In early 1820, eleven states were considered free or Northern states and eleven were considered slave or Southern states. The Northern states had a much larger population than the Southern states did. Many immigrants wanted to live in the North because of the job opportunities there. The Industrial Revolution had left its mark on the North—factories and businesses abounded.

The Southern economy depended upon agriculture. The invention of Eli Whitney's cotton gin made cotton a practical and profitable crop. In fact, it became the South's largest cash crop. "Cotton is king!" became a popular saying in the South.

The successful cultivation of cotton depended upon a large labor force. The work was hard and tiring, but cultivation didn't require skilled labor. The plantations of the South covered vast areas of land. The labor requirement directly increased with the amount of land to be worked. Slave labor appeared to be the backbone of the Southern economy.

1. Why was the preservation of slavery important to many people living in the South? _____
_____
_____
_____

2. What did the phrase "Cotton is king!" mean? _____
_____
_____

3. The number of representatives a state has in the House of Representatives is determined by the state's population. In the Senate, there are two representatives per state. During the time period just before the Civil War, do you think Southern politicians concentrated more on influencing the representatives in the House or in the Senate? Why?
_____
_____
_____

The Missouri Compromise

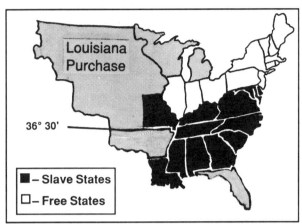

Louisiana Purchase

36° 30'

■ – Slave States
□ – Free States

In 1818, the territory of Missouri requested admittance to the Union as a slave state. Since eleven free states and eleven slave states were represented in Congress at that time, Missouri's entrance as a slave state would have upset the balance. A compromise was offered by New York congressman James Tallmadge. It stated that Missouri could enter as a slave state, but had to emancipate its slaves when they reached twenty-five years of age. It also stated that no additional slaves could enter Missouri and children born to existing Missouri slaves would be considered free. This bill passed in the House, but failed in the Senate.

Soon Maine requested admittance to the Union as a free state. Henry Clay, later called the "Great Compromiser," suggested a compromise. He proposed that Missouri and Maine enter the Union at the same time. Missouri would enter as a slave state, and Maine would enter as a free state. He added that from then on, no slavery would be allowed in the remaining sections of the Louisiana Purchase north of the 36° 30' north parallel.

The Missouri Compromise, which was later amended, passed. It stood for thirty-seven years, until the Supreme Court nullified it in the Dred Scott decision.

1. What does the word *emancipate* mean? _____

   _____

2. Why do you think the Southern states would not accept Tallmadge's
   proposal? _____

   _____

   _____

3. Why did both the North and the South attempt to keep a balance of free
   and slave states represented in Congress? _____

   _____

   _____

4. Why would Maine's request to enter the Union as a free state have caused
   the North to breathe a sigh of relief? _____

   _____

   _____

The Dred Scott Decision

Dred Scott was a Missouri slave. In 1834, his master took him to Illinois (a free state) and the Wisconsin Territory (a free territory) for a period of four years. Then Scott and his master returned to Missouri (a slave state). Scott felt that because he had lived in areas where slavery was illegal, he was free and, therefore, could no longer be held as a slave. In 1846, Scott brought suit against his owners, contending that he was a free man. The case was tried in Missouri and Scott won. However, the decision was reversed by Missouri's Supreme Court. Scott appealed the case until it reached the United States Supreme Court.

At this time the Supreme Court leaned toward Southern interests. In fact, the Chief Justice, Roger Taney, was adamantly pro-South. Because of this, the Court upheld the Missouri Supreme Court ruling and Dred Scott's request for freedom was refused. The U.S. Supreme Court stated that Illinois law did not affect the laws in Missouri, where Scott was residing at the time of the ruling. Therefore, Scott was still considered a slave. Furthermore, the Court said, because slaves were not United States citizens, they could not bring suit in court. Finally, the Court reasoned that because slaves were property, their status was protected by the Fifth Amendment of the Constitution, which protects a citizen's right to own property. This meant that Congress did not have the power to outlaw slavery in any part of the United States. This decision, passed down in 1857, made the Missouri Compromise, which had forbidden slavery in the remaining parts of the Louisiana Purchase north of the 36° 30' parallel, unconstitutional and illegal.

1. Explain how the ruling in the Dred Scott case made the Missouri Compromise unconstitutional.

   _____

   _____

   _____

2. Pretend that you are Chief Justice of the Supreme Court during the Dred Scott case. Write your decision on the lines below and explain why you've decided in this manner. Continue writing on the back of this paper.

   _____

   _____

   _____

   _____

   _____

   _____

John Brown at Harper's Ferry

By the late 1850's tensions were running high between the North and South. In Congress, eighteen free states and fifteen slave states were represented. Many in the South felt that slavery could not be protected or expanded unless the Southern states seceded from the Union and formed their own country.

One of the reasons for the South's confidence that Southerners could form a separate and successful country was the European need for cotton. The South felt that European nations had become dependent upon Southern cotton for their growing textile industries. England, in particular, was thought to be a strong supporter of Southern interests. In fact, throughout the Civil War, the South continued to strive for help from both France and England.

Amid suspicion and growing secessionist feeling came an event that further split the nation. John Brown, an ardent abolitionist, had devised a plan he felt would provoke Southern slaves into revolt. He and a small band of men planned to take over a Federal arsenal at Harper's Ferry, Virginia, on October 16, 1859. His hope was to arm slaves with guns and ammunition from the arsenal and spark a revolution.

United States Marines, under the command of Robert E. Lee, greeted Brown and his followers. Brown and his men were captured and the anticipated slave uprising was prevented. Later, following a trial, Brown was hanged for treason and murder. To many in the North, John Brown was a hero and a martyr.

Brown's uprising never came about, but his act planted the fear of a slave uprising in many Southern hearts. The nation moved closer to war.

1. What was one reason that Southerners felt they could form a successful nation if they left the Union? _____

_____

_____

2. How did the events at Harper's Ferry affect the North and the South?

_____

_____

_____

3. Do you think John Brown was a hero? Why or why not? _____

_____

_____

_____

Secession

In 1860 the Southern way of life was seriously threatened. Personal liberty laws, enacted by the North in opposition to the Fugitive Slave Law, were the result of increasing abolitionist sentiment. (The Fugitive Slave Act of 1850 stipulated that warrants could be issued for the arrest of runaway slaves, even if slaves were apprehended in free territories. It also imposed heavy punishment on anyone who helped a runaway slave or attempted to prevent the return of a slave to his or her master.) Harriet Beecher Stowe's book entitled *Uncle Tom's Cabin* openly criticized slavery. Abraham Lincoln, who represented the anti-slavery Republicans, won the presidency. Southerners grew increasingly sure that slavery would be abolished if they did not act quickly.

Lincoln was to take office on March 4, 1861. The existing president, James Buchanan, was not viewed as a strong president. He had not made a definite statement about whether or not he would force Southern states back into the Union if they seceded. Some Southerners felt that if the South seceded, the North had no reason to retaliate. After all, they thought, Southerners were not trying to change the North, they simply wanted to maintain the Southern lifestyle.

Before Lincoln took office, while Buchanan was still president, South Carolina met in convention. The topic on the agenda was secession from the Union. On December 20, 1860, South Carolina formally seceded. Soon Alabama, Georgia, Florida, Louisiana, Mississippi, and Texas followed. Buchanan did not respond with force. The Confederacy was born on February 8, 1861, with the adoption of a constitution and the election of Jefferson Davis as president and Alexander Stephens as vice-president.

1. Why do you think South Carolina seceded when it did?

    _____

    _____

    _____

2. What do you think Southern plantation owners at the South Carolina convention in December 1860 had to say on the issue of secession?

    _____

    _____

    _____

    _____

War Begins at Fort Sumter

Following South Carolina's secession, the state demanded that Northern troops be removed from Fort Sumter. The newly inaugurated Abraham Lincoln was faced with a dilemma—he wanted the troops to remain in South Carolina *and* he wanted to preserve all the good will and negotiating power he could with the South. Lincoln decided to send supplies to the fort and head the convoy with a small group of naval vessels. In an attempt to keep from angering the South, Lincoln sent word to the governor of South Carolina that provisions were being sent to the fort.

In mid-April, 1861, the South's Brigadier General P.G.T. Beauregard sent a note by ship to the commanding Northern officer, Major Robert Anderson, formally demanding that Fort Sumter be surrendered. Major Anderson declined, and at 4:30 A.M. on April 12, 1861, the first shots of the Civil War rang out as Southern troops fired on Fort Sumter.

In the ensuing bombardment, few casualties were suffered. The shelling continued until Anderson's surrender on April 13. Northern forces were allowed to march out of the fort and board a ship to return to the North. This first battle of the Civil War was fought in a "gentlemanly" fashion, but it preceded a bloody war that cost many lives from both the North and the South.

1. Why did South Carolina feel it could demand that Northern troops be withdrawn from Fort Sumter? _____
_____
_____

2. Why did Lincoln inform South Carolina that he was sending supplies to Fort Sumter? _____
_____
_____

3. If you had been Lincoln, would you have acted differently? Write what you would have done and why. _____
_____
_____
_____

4. How else could South Carolina have responded to the sending of reinforcements to Fort Sumter? _____
_____
_____
_____

The North and South Compared

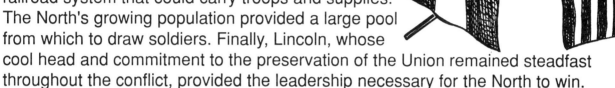

During the Civil War period, the North and South were different in many ways. Their economies, lifestyles, military might, and war capabilities differed. The North was industrialized and already possessed the factories needed to produce the ammunition and weapons to carry on a war. It also had a strong railroad system that could carry troops and supplies. The North's growing population provided a large pool from which to draw soldiers. Finally, Lincoln, whose cool head and commitment to the preservation of the Union remained steadfast throughout the conflict, provided the leadership necessary for the North to win.

Though the South's capital, Richmond, Virginia, was equipped with iron-working plants that could provide war supplies, the Southern economy was agrarian; most of its people worked on farms. However, the South did have some advantages. It had a good stock of military men, most notably the brilliant strategist Robert E. Lee. Southern troops were very familiar with most of the land where the fighting would take place, and many were also skilled horsemen who knew well the ways of the outdoors.

1. What, in your opinion, was the South's biggest advantage in the Civil War? What was the South's biggest disadvantage? Why do you think so?

_____

_____

_____

_____

_____

_____

2. What, in your opinion, was the North's biggest advantage in the Civil War? What was the North's biggest disadvantage? Why do you think so?

_____

_____

_____

_____

_____

_____

Map of the Union and the Confederacy

1. Label the states on the map. (Shaded areas are territories.)
2. Mark each state Union (U) or Confederate (C).
3. Draw a star on the first state to secede from the Union.
4. Trace the boundary between Union and Confederate states.

Use pg 483

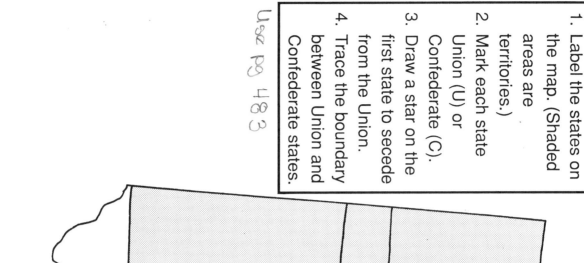

The Clash of the Ironclads

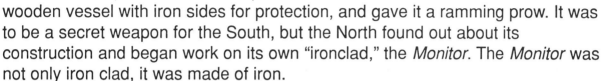

The Confederate ironclad ship called the *Merrimack* began its life as an American navy vessel. Union troops had sunk the ship when they abandoned the Norfolk, Virginia, navy yard after the start of the Civil War. Confederate troops raised it, and renamed it the *Virginia.* (As in the text that follows, the ship is often referred to by its original name, the *Merrimack.*) Confederate troops refitted the wooden vessel with iron sides for protection, and gave it a ramming prow. It was to be a secret weapon for the South, but the North found out about its construction and began work on its own "ironclad," the *Monitor.* The *Monitor* was not only iron clad, it was made of iron.

The *Merrimack* showed its worth in the destruction of two Union warships. She also ran three ships aground off the coast of Virginia. The *Monitor* steamed to the rescue of the Union fleet and on March 9, 1862, a battle between the two ships commenced in Hampton Roads, a channel of water just off the coast of Virginia. The smaller ship, the *Monitor,* moved quickly compared to the *Merrimack.* But neither ship's guns harmed the other, so protected were they by their new fittings. In the end, after several hours of fighting, the battle ended in a stalemate; neither ship won.

Unfortunately, by the end of 1862 both ships met a sad end. When Norfolk was captured by Union troops, the Confederates blew up the *Merrimack* rather than let her be captured by the North. The *Monitor* sank during a storm on the last day of the year, 1862.

1. Why do you think the stalemate between the *Merrimack* and the *Monitor* was considered by many to be a Union victory?

   _____

   _____

   _____

2. Imagine that you are a newspaper reporter. Write a story about "The Battle of Hampton Roads." Continue your article on another sheet of paper.

   _____

   _____

   _____

   _____

The Emancipation Proclamation

That on the first day of January, in the year of our Lord one thousand eight hundred and sixty-three, all persons held as slaves within any State, or designated part of a State, the people whereof shall then be in rebellion against the United States, shall be then, thenceforward, and forever free; and the Executive Government of the United States, including the military and naval authority thereof, will recognize and maintain the freedom of such persons, and will do no act or acts to repress such person, or any of them, in any efforts they may make for their actual freedom.

The text above is part of a document which changed the course of United States history, the Emancipation Proclamation. The Emancipation Proclamation, issued by President Abraham Lincoln on January 1, 1863, declared that all slaves in Confederate territories at war against the Union were free. This document played a role in the North's success in the Civil War.

Before the Emancipation Proclamation, Southern slaves kept many Southern factories and farms in production while Confederate soldiers went to war. After Lincoln issued the proclamation, thousands of newly freed Southern slaves headed north. Many of them joined Union troops in the fight to abolish slavery.

The Emancipation Proclamation did not abolish slavery in all slave states. Four Union states—Kentucky, Missouri, Delaware, and Maryland— remained slave states. Lincoln feared that if he banned slavery in these states, they would join the other slave states in seceding from the Union.

The terms of the Emancipation Proclamation were created as wartime policies and were not considered to be permanent. Because of this, Lincoln devoted himself to supporting passage of the 13th Amendment, which permanently abolished slavery in the United States.

1. How did the Emancipation Proclamation solve the problem of decreasing enlistment in the Union army and navy?

   _____

   _____

   _____

2. How do you think Southern plantation owners reacted to the Emancipation Proclamation? _____

   _____

   _____

   _____

   _____

The Gettysburg Address

A famous and important battle fought in Union territory took place in Gettysburg, Pennsylvania, from July 1 through July 3, 1863. It pitted General George G. Meade against the South's premier military strategist, Robert E. Lee. Lee lost almost one third of his troops, an estimated 28,000 men, during this battle.

Lee was attempting to bring his troops together at Gettysburg, and Meade was determined to prevent it. Union troops established a position south of Gettysburg. Lee unsuccessfully attacked the flanks of the Union troops, then, in a last effort, sent 15,000 of General George E. Pickett's infantrymen, line by line, into the fire of Union guns and cannons. Half of Pickett's men were lost. Lee retreated to Virginia to mend his troops. Meade, though urged by President Lincoln to follow and hopefully finish off the Confederates, chose not to chase Lee and his battle-weary troops.

Lincoln's three minute Gettysburg address, reproduced below, was delivered at the November 1863 dedication of a cemetery resting on the battlefield's site.

The Gettysburg Address

Four score and seven years ago our fathers brought forth on this continent, a new nation, conceived in Liberty, and dedicated to the proposition that all men are created equal.

Now we are engaged in a great civil war, testing whether that nation or any nation so conceived and so dedicated can long endure. We are met on a great battlefield of that war. We have come to dedicate a portion of that field, as a final resting place for those who here gave their lives that that nation might live. It is altogether fitting and proper that we should do this.

But, in a larger sense, we cannot dedicate—we cannot consecrate—we cannot hallow—this ground. The brave men, living and dead, who struggled here have consecrated it, far above our poor power to add or detract. The world will little note, nor long remember what we say here, but it can never forget what they did here. It is for us the living, rather, to be dedicated here to the unfinished work which they who fought here have thus far so nobly advanced. It is rather for us to be here dedicated to the great task remaining before us—that from these honored dead we take increased devotion to that cause for which they gave the last full measure of devotion—that we here highly resolve that these dead shall not have died in vain—that this nation, under God, shall have a new birth of freedom—and that government of the people, by the people, for the people, shall not perish from the earth.

The Gettysburg Address

1. When was the cemetery at Gettysburg dedicated? _____

2. In the second paragraph of Lincoln's address, he said that the Civil War tested whether or not a nation dedicated to the idea that all men are created equal could endure. What do you think he meant by this?

   _____

   _____

   _____

   _____

3. What did Lincoln mean when he said that those who had died at Gettysburg could not be allowed to have died in vain?

   _____

   _____

   _____

4. Explain how the United States is a government "of the people, by the people, for the people." _____

   _____

   _____

   _____

   _____

5. What is the name for such a government? _____

6. Why do you think Lincoln was adamant about bringing the South back into the Union? _____

   _____

   _____

   _____

   _____

7. How do you think the United States would be different today if Lincoln had not taken a strong stand to abolish slavery and bring the South back into the Union? Why? _____

   _____

   _____

   _____

The Underground Railroad

During the Civil War period, a series of secret passages leading from the South to Northern cities and Canada was established to help slaves escape from slavery. These roads to freedom were referred to as the Underground Railroad. The heroic people who helped the slaves along these dangerous routes provided guidance, shelter, food, and clothing.

One of the most remarkable heroines of the Underground Railroad was Harriet Tubman, a slave born in Bucktown, Maryland. An escaped slave herself, Tubman made nineteen trips back to the South and led countless slaves to freedom. She was known as "Moses," a courageous woman who led people to freedom.

When Harriet Tubman decided to escape, she found no one, neither family nor friends, who would accompany her on such a dangerous trip. She left everything she had known—family, friends, and her home. She traveled alone, following paths she thought would lead her to the North.

After settling in Philadelphia, Harriet returned to the South, gathering companies of brave slaves whose confidence in Tubman was well-founded. She led countless people to freedom. Each trip south, became increasingly dangerous for Tubman. The more her reputation spread, the more pro-slavery people tried to stop her. Still Tubman continued to lead slaves north and help them adjust to their new lifestyle. After her death, Harriet Tubman was buried in Auburn, New York, where she had settled her aging parents after leading them to freedom.

Pretend you are escaping to the North with Harriet Tubman. In a small journal that you bring along, you write notes on what your first night of freedom feels like. What do you hope for? What are you afraid of? Write your notes below. Continue your writing on the back of this paper.

_____

_____

_____

_____

_____

_____

_____

_____

Lincoln's Reelection

By 1864, both the North and South had wearied of the long and bloody war. Lincoln was running for reelection and was opposed by George B. McClellan, the Democratic candidate. Most people believed that if McClellan was elected, he would agree to a peaceful end to the conflict. Because of his indecisiveness on the battlefield, however, it was doubtful that McClellan would take the strong stand Lincoln had taken for bringing the Southern states back into the Union.

By November 1864, however, the North's confidence in the war effort had increased. On March 9, 1864, Lincoln had given Ulysses S. Grant charge of all Union troops—an act that sealed the South's defeat. Successful campaigns had been waged by General Phillip H. Sheridan in the Shenandoah Valley and by General William T. Sherman in Georgia. Sheridan's troops had defeated Confederate troops in the Shenandoah Valley, destroying anything that might be of use to the Confederacy. In September, Sherman had captured Atlanta by defeating Confederate troops led by General John Hood.

These victories gave the North the boost they needed. Lincoln was reelected and Northern troops continued to take steps toward a Civil War victory.

1. What factors led to Lincoln's reelection in 1864?

    _____

    _____

    _____

    _____

2. What doubts did people have about George McClellan? Do you think these doubts were well founded? Why or why not?

    _____

    _____

    _____

    _____

3. Who do you think would have won the 1864 presidential election if the North had not been successful in battle during the time period just before the election? Why? _____

    _____

    _____

    _____

Surrender at Appomattox Court House

Shortly after Abraham Lincoln's second inauguration, which took place on March 4, 1865, General Grant attempted to capture Richmond, Virginia. He hounded General Lee and his troops, fighting several times. In April of 1865, Grant and his troops took over the railroad in the area. While Grant's troops received supplies, and equipment, Lee's troops were battered, hungry, and fatigued. Each time the two armies met, both Grant and Lee sustained heavy losses, but Grant, unlike previous Union leaders, refused to pull back to refresh his troops. He kept close on the heels of Lee.

Eventually, Lee realized his troops could no longer go on. He asked to meet with Grant. The two met in Appomattox Court House, Virginia, on April 9, 1865, to finalize the terms of surrender. General Grant was generous. When Lee pointed out that the Southern troops had brought their own horses into battle, Grant allowed the Confederate troops to keep the horses. Grant also ordered that Lee's troops be immediately fed. Though General Sherman had yet to receive the surrender of Confederate General Albert Johnston in North Carolina, the Civil War, for all practical purposes, was over.

1. Grant's idea to have Union troops persist in attacking without stopping to rest or reorganize was new to Civil War strategy. Do you think it was a good idea? Why or why not? _____

   _____

   _____

2. Why do you think it was important for the Southern troops to keep their horses after the war? (Hint: Think about the Southern economy at that time.) _____

   _____

   _____

3. What reasons might General Grant have had for being so generous in the agreement he made with General Lee upon surrender?

   _____

   _____

   _____

Lincoln's Assassination

Lincoln's inaugural address in 1864 closed with these lines:

> With malice toward none, with charity for all, with firmness in the right as God gives us to see the right, let us strive on to finish the work we are in, to bind up the nation's wounds, to care for him who shall have borne the battle and for his widow and his orphan, to do all which may achieve and cherish a just and lasting peace among ourselves and with all nations.

Lincoln had anticipated a Northern victory and had begun making plans to "reconstruct" the South. He had already set a charitable precedent in dealing with three former Confederate states—Tennessee, Louisiana and Arkansas—which returned to Union control in 1863. Lincoln allowed them to revive their state governments and reenter the Union when ten percent of the voters swore loyalty to the United States. He pardoned almost all of their citizens. It was clear that Lincoln's attitude towards the South and Reconstruction was lenient; however Lincoln's merciful vision of Reconstruction was not to be.

On April 14, 1865, Lincoln and his wife, Mary Todd, were seated at Ford's Theatre in Washington, watching a play. An actor, John Wilkes Booth, entered their box and shot President Lincoln at close range. Lincoln died the next evening. A division of the Republican Party called the Radical Republicans took charge of Reconstruction. They believed Southern states should be treated like conquered territories, and that Congress had the right to decide all new policies in these states. An attitude of punishment and feelings of anger governed an era that Lincoln had so hoped would be filled with forgiveness and the healing of a nation's wounds.

1. What do the lines from Lincoln's inaugural address tell you about his attitude towards reconstructing the Union? _____

    _____

    _____

2. How would you have dealt with the Confederate states after the Civil War? What provisions would you have made for their reentry into the Union?

    _____

    _____

    _____

    _____

    _____

    _____